WRESTLING SUPERST★RS

MARK HENRY

BY JESSE ARMSTRONG

EPIC

BELLWETHER MEDIA • MINNEAPOLIS, MN

EPIC

EPIC BOOKS are no ordinary books. They burst with intense action, high-speed heroics, and shadows of the unknown. Are you ready for an Epic adventure?

This edition first published in 2015 by Bellwether Media, Inc.

No part of this publication may be reproduced in whole or in part without written permission of the publisher. For information regarding permission, write to Bellwether Media, Inc., Attention: Permissions Department, 5357 Penn Avenue South, Minneapolis, MN 55419.

Library of Congress Cataloging-in-Publication Data

Armstrong, Jesse.
  Mark Henry / by Jesse Armstrong.
    pages cm. – (Epic. Wrestling Superstars)
  Includes bibliographical references and index.
  Summary: "Engaging images accompany information about Mark Henry. The combination of high-interest subject matter and light text is intended for students in grades 2 through 7"– Provided by publisher.
  Audience: Ages 7-12.
  ISBN 978-1-62617-181-7 (hardcover : alk. paper)
  1. Henry, Mark, 1971–Juvenile literature. 2. Wrestlers–United States–Biography–Juvenile literature. I. Title.
  GV1196.H48A75 2015
  796.812092–dc23
  [B]
                        2014034781

Printed in the United States of America, North Mankato, MN.

TABLE OF CONTENTS

WARNING!

The wrestling moves used in this book are performed by professionals. Do not attempt to reenact any of the moves performed in this book.

THE DEBUT

Jerry "The King" Lawler puts Mark Henry in a headlock. However, Henry fights back with a counter move. Henry may not have experience. But he has size and strength.

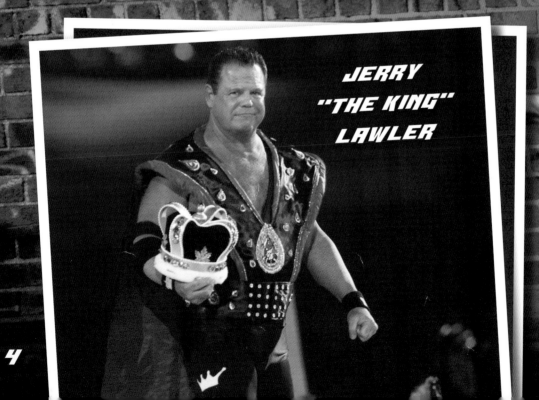

JERRY "THE KING" LAWLER

Henry throws Lawler around the ring. Soon Lawler is defeated. Other wrestlers attack Henry after the win. But they do not wreck his debut.

WHO IS MARK HENRY?

★

In 2002, Henry was the strongest man in the world. He won the Arnold Strongman Classic.

Mark Henry is the strongest man in WWE.
He uses his power to crush his opponents.
His muscles usually give him the edge.

LIFE BEFORE WWE

Henry was 200 pounds (91 kilograms) by age 10. At school, bullies picked on him because of his weight. He started powerlifting and playing football to gain respect.

Eventually Henry became one of the world's best athletes. He competed in the Olympics in 1992 and 1996. He was a member of the U.S. men's weightlifting team.

FIRST A FAN

★

Henry was a WWE fan long before becoming a wrestler. He watched the events on Monday nights and on the weekends.

A WWE SUPERSTAR

WRESTLING NAME:	Mark Henry
REAL NAME:	Mark Jerrold Henry
BIRTHDATE:	June 12, 1971
HOMETOWN:	Silsbee, Texas
HEIGHT:	6 feet, 4 inches (1.9 meters)
WEIGHT:	412 pounds (187 kilograms)
WWE DEBUT:	1996
FINISHING MOVE:	World's Strongest Slam

Henry joined WWE after the 1996 Olympics. His weightlifting success earned him an invite to the ring. He started wrestling as a face.

Over the years, Henry has overpowered some of WWE's largest superstars. In 2008, he beat Big Show and Kane in a Triple Threat Match. This win came with a major title.

BIG SHOW

KANE

★

Big Daddy V and The Great Khali are other giants Henry has defeated.

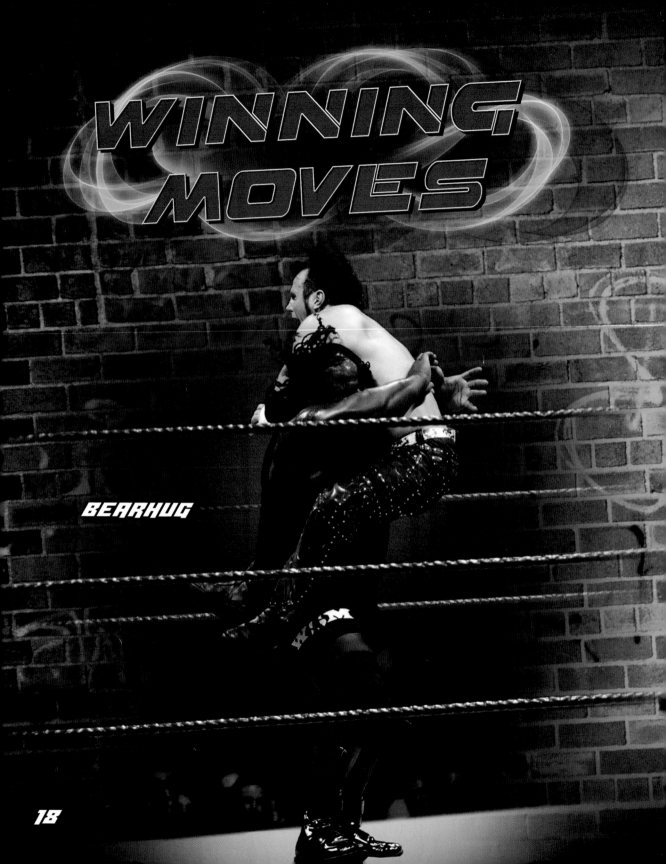

WINNING MOVES

BEARHUG

BODY AVALANCHE

Henry often traps an opponent in a Bearhug.
This signature move is a strong squeeze.
He also corners opponents with the Body
Avalanche. They are buried under his weight.

The World's Strongest Slam is his
finishing move. Henry lifts an opponent up
to his chest. Then he falls forward. He slams
the wrestler into the mat. It is crushing!

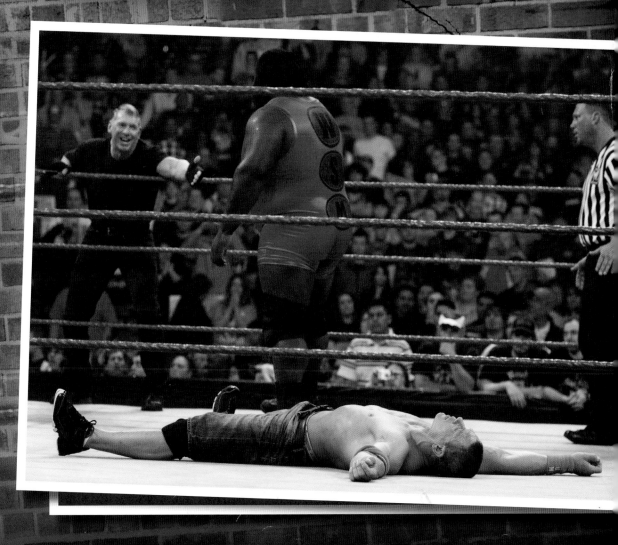

GLOSSARY

avalanche—a large amount of snow and rocks falling down a mountain

counter move—a move that is a response to another move

debut—first official appearance

face—a wrestler viewed as a hero

finishing move—a wrestling move that finishes off an opponent

Olympics—a gathering every four years in which the world's best athletes compete for medals

powerlifting—a sport that tests strength through three lifts; the lifts are the bench press, squat, and dead lift.

signature move—a move that a wrestler is famous for performing

title—championship

Triple Threat Match—a match involving three wrestlers at the same time

TO LEARN MORE

At the Library

Armstrong, Jesse. *Big Show*. Minneapolis, Minn.: Bellwether Media, 2015.

Black, Jake. *WWE General Manager's Handbook*. New York, N.Y.: Grosset & Dunlap, 2012.

West, Tracey. *Race to the Rumble*. New York, N.Y.: Grosset & Dunlap, 2011.

On the Web

Learning more about Mark Henry is as easy as 1, 2, 3.

1. Go to www.factsurfer.com.

2. Enter "Mark Henry" into the search box.

3. Click the "Surf" button and you will see a list of related web sites.

With factsurfer.com, finding more information is just a click away.

INDEX

The images in this book are reproduced through the courtesy of: Ethan Miller/ Getty Images, front cover; Chris Ryan/ Corbis, front cover (small), pp. 16 (left), 20, 21; Miguel Pereira/ Alamy, pp. 4-5; Matt Roberts/ Zuma Press/ Newscom, p. 4 (small); George Napolitano/ Corbis, pp. 6-7; Kevan Brooks/ AdMedia/ Newscom, p. 8; Panoramic/ Zuma Press/ Newscom, p. 9; David Seto, pp. 10, 11; Mike King/ Corbis, p. 12; Zuma Press/ Newscom, p. 13; Moses Robinson/ Getty Images, pp. 14, 17; Michael Buckner/ Getty Images, p. 16 (right); Alexandre Pona/ City Files/ Icon SMI/ Newscom, p. 18.